Now there are varieties
of gifts,
    but the same Spirit;
and there are varieties
of service,
    but the same Lord;
and there are varieties
of activities,
    but it is the same God
who empowers them all
in everyone.

1 Corinthians 12:4–6

 Published by Concordia Publishing House
3558 S. Jefferson Avenue, St. Louis, MO 63118-3968
1-800-325-3040 ▪ www.cph.org

Manufactured in Shenzhen, China/022100/300484

1   2   3   4   5   6   7   8   9   10   22   21   20   19   18   17   16   15   14   13

How Can I Help?
GOD'S CALLING FOR KIDS

By Mary J. Moerbe

with Gene Edward Veith

Illustrated by

Jennifer Zivoin

CONCORDIA PUBLISHING HOUSE • SAINT LOUIS

For Parents

Being a child is a vocation, a calling from God. Not only that, Luther said that a little boy doing what his parents say or a little girl doing her chores is doing a holier work than that of the strictest monks or nuns ("The Fourth Commandment," The Large Catechism).

How can that be? Because Christian children have faith and live out that faith in their everyday lives where God has placed them, just as their parents do.

When we hear the word *vocation*, we think about jobs and how we make our living, but the word literally means "calling." Paul summarizes the doctrine of vocation: "Only let each person lead the life that the Lord has assigned to him, and to which God has called him" (1 Corinthians 7:17).

We have been "called" by the Gospel, as the Small Catechism says, something that first happened in Baptism. God "assigns" us to different spheres of life and "calls" us to them through the course of our lives. Christians have multiple vocations: in the workplace, but also in the church (as in our "called and ordained" pastors); in the society (as citizens); and in the family (as husbands and wives, fathers and mothers, sons and daughters).

The purpose of every vocation is to love and serve our neighbors. Our relationship with God is based solely on His love for us in Christ, but then He sends us out into our everyday callings to love and to help the people He brings into our lives through our various callings (1 John 4:7–21).

So this applies to baptized children as well!

Their world is much smaller than an adult's, but they, too, are learning to serve in church (going to Sunday School and worship services), in the society (learning to be well-behaved in public), in their future workplace (developing their talents and beginning their education), and—most important for them—in the family (learning to honor their parents and to get along with their neighbors, who are their brothers or sisters).

Luther taught that God is present in all vocations, and they are grounded in Him (marriage manifests Christ and the Church, parenthood is grounded in our heavenly Father, childhood rests in the Son of God). Furthermore, God Himself works through vocations. He gives us our daily bread through farmers and bakers. He heals us through doctors and nurses. He protects us through police officers and firefighters. He creates and cares for children through mothers and fathers.

This means that God is present in children and works through children as well!

We parents know how much God blesses us through our children, how they pull love out of us, force us into responsibility, and turn us into adults.

Part of the vocation of being a parent is to help our children grow up into callings of their own. This book is designed to help with that. It is written by my daughter. She and I collaborated on a book entitled *Family Vocation: God's Calling in Marriage, Parenthood, and Childhood*. How happy she makes me to see how God is working through her in her various callings as a deaconess, a wife, a mother, and a writer!

Being a child is the only vocation that everyone has (since everyone has been born). And though children grow up into adults, they will always be sons or daughters of their parents. Those vocations are permanent. And as Christians, we are all permanently God's children.

Parents are called to love and serve their children, and children are called to love and serve their parents. Both will be asking each other all of their lives, "How can I help?"

Gene Edward Veith

God is the greatest helper.

He is so great He never needs help!

God may not
need help,
but I do.

God gives
me people
in my life
so we can
share His
gifts.

God gives us
our daily
bread,
but my
mom and dad
help me
to receive it.

My parents
and family
help me.
So do many
others!

I am glad
God helps me
through them.

God helps me through people who provide what I need to be healthy.

Sometimes, I'd rather have something else, but today I'm still learning to listen to my parents.

People help me.
I help others
too!

Everybody
needs help.

I help when I obey my parents.

And sometimes, I help without knowing it because God works through me.

Every day I
grow into new
ways to help.

God will
always work
through me.

When I grow up, I will help others on a farm or in an office or wherever I will be.

I can get married and have children, and I will help them too!

Every day, God works through people.

Every day, God works through His Son!

Jesus is much more than a helper. He is my Savior.

He gives me life and faith. He forgives me when I do wrong things.

Thank You, God, for saving me and being the Greatest Helper.

Thank You for all Your gifts and for letting me help others.

Amen.

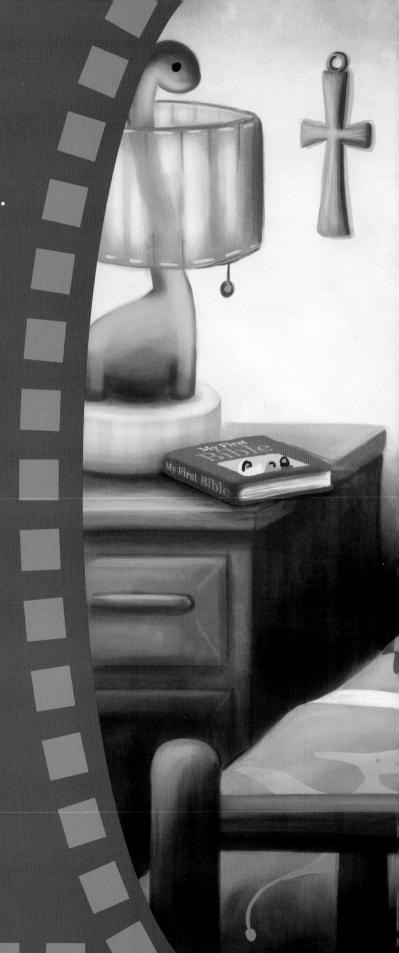